Mark Rozen Pettinelli

<u>Garlic</u> low blood pressure, high cholesterol
heart disease, rectal cancer, lung cancer
diabetes, osteoarthritis, yeast infections, tick bites
fish, swine flu tick bites mosquito repellent
common cold, bacterial and fungal infections
earaches, shortness of breath, snake bites
death in one bloody diarrhea, bloody urine
whooping cough, tooth sensitive warts

<u>Ginger</u> morning sickness, upset stomach
gas, diarrhea irritable bowel sore
nausea rheumatoid arthritis
insect bites, headache trouble sleeping
toothaches bleeding colds, flu
lots of appetite, itching

Mark Roton Peddinelli

<u>astragalus</u>

heart failure, diabetes
protect liver, fight bacteria, viruses
wound healing   allergies, chest pain
vision problems for people with diabetes

<u>Monner root (baji tian)</u>

cancer, gallbladder disorders, helps
strengthens endocrine system

<u>He Shou Wu</u>   cancer
aging, chronic disease   anti-viral
protect liver diabetes heart health
cholesterol   cognition + focus hair growth

<u>berberine</u>

diabetes, high cholesterol
stronger heart beats   the body
controls sugar   lowers sugar metabolism
glaucoma   low blood platelets counts

Mark Xiornik Rozen Pettinelli

Benefits I Get from the following:

Resveratrol: heart disease
clear arteries atherosclerosis   muscle growth
glucose and lipid metabolism
increased blood flow to the brain
helps diabetes by reducing complications
  improve energy and endurance
    prevents cancer   helps fight infections
  Glucose balance
heart health   fungal, viral and bacterial

Acetyl L-Carnitine: liver function
                      brain function
reduce fatigue   improve performance
help insulin resistance
protective against heart disease   blood flow to
                                    the brain
kidney function, bones
nerve pain related to diabetes

primrose oil!   arthritis, weak bones
cancer, high cholesterol, heart disease

nerve damage related to diabetes

MVM xanth Rosa petalnoids

<u>krill oil</u>: supports strong bones and joints
decrease risk of heart disease and
improvements in cardiovascular function
decreas risk improving   skin texture and
brain health   moisture

<u>pterostilbene</u>: high cholesterol
blood suga (glucose) diabetes / levels
injury response

peanut grain: supports bone health
digestive system   source of protein
lowers cholesterol brain food

Mark Rozen Pettinelli

<u>Maca</u> energy, athletic performance
memory, infertility

<u>eleuthero</u> reduce edema
energy, inflammation, blood flow to
cancer, healing wounds
increase low blood pressure, breast...
respiratory tract, infections
nerve damage, blood sugar levels

<u>ashwagandha</u>
ADHD, anxiety, ... stress
stress, fibromyalgia, asthma, ...
brain, fibro, myalgia, ...
liver disease, parkinsons ...
thinking ability

Mark Rozen Pettinelli

Fenugreek

inflammation of the stomach   diabetes
poor thyroid function   kidney disease
high cholesterol
mouth ulcers, boils, bronchitis
chronic coughs, chapped lips, baldness
exercise performance, heartburn

hypothe A - Chinese club moss

alertness and energy, loss of mental alertness

Holy basil

Cold/flu   dental plaque   tuberculosis
earache, bronchitis   diabetes   malaria
viral hepatitis
mercury poisoning   ring worm, ...

Rhodiola   strength

hearing loss
irregular heartbeat

Mark Rocco Pettinelli

Benefits of supplements

<u>Psyllum</u>
reduce high cholesterol, blood sugar
   constipation, diarrhea
   weight loss   strengthen heart muscle

<u>Fish oil</u>
   cholesterol levels, clogged arteries, chest pain
   irregular heart beat
      kidney failure   "brain food"

   dry eyes, glaucoma, macular degeneration
   exercise performance, diabetes, asthma
   bones+joints   gum disease

<u>Cranberry</u>
   kidneys, colds, flu, indigestion
   wound healing

<u>Cissus</u>   bone health, burns fat
diabetes, bacterial infections, high cholesterol
tendrils, control diabetes
protects the liver
               wound healing

Mark Pettinelli

So I'm trying to figure it out?
is there anything special about
feelings and emotions?

I've already pointed out the difference
between feelings and emotions...
feelings are things you feel like touch, taste
and smell

while emotions are deep and powerful
like love, hate, happy, sad or disgust

emotions are important because they
move us and motivate us
while feelings are more simply
things we can feel

So that brings up the question:
is there anything special about
feelings? or emotions?

well, there certainly isn't anything
special about thoughts, but there
might be something special about
feelings.

Mark Pettinelli

Mark Kettinelli

So feelings are important
I want to have a lot of feelings
the only question is - what do I
want to feel?

I mean I could get a girlfriend
that might be fun

but there's other ways to have
fun in life I think

watching movies is fun, or just
regular television

I like interacting with people I mean
I've been interacting with people
my whole life at this point

maybe I need to think more
about this, I mean I think
I've already finished my analysis
on emotions and feelings...

Mark Kettinelli

Mark Petterelli

What else would I need to analyze?

I mean I've figured out just about everything I would need to know

I know how to keep track of my emotions and thoughts

I know that I have feelings and thoughts

thoughts are extremely important
so are feelings, so my question is—
what else would I need to know
other than how to keep track
of my own feelings and thoughts

emotions are stronger then feelings
any strong feeling can be an emotion
but that is just the definition of
the words feeling and emotion

they mean basically the same thing—
and can even be used interchangeably

Mark Petterelli

Mark Kettrelli

So I've already pointed out
that I can keep track of
my emotions and thoughts

I don't know if I need to be
able to do anything else

I'm fairly happy with myself
however all I can seem to do
is keep track of my emotions and
thoughts

I have a steady stream of feelings
that comes from my emotions
I also think about stuff

I'm fairly satisfied with my life
I don't have panic attacks even
though I went to the ER
emergency room a bunch of times
recently for freaking out

Mark Kettrelli

Mark Kettnells

I've had a long life at this point
it's been many years since I was born
I'm going to turn 36 years old soon
thats a long time a

I try to stay in the moment with
a steady stream of feelings and thoughts

I've been reading with therapists
who talk to their patients about
feelings and thoughts

I've also reviewed ~~and~~ many
cognitive psychology textbooks,
and also books on emotion and cognition

If you think about it emotion and
reason are the two most critical
mental processes

I mean, either you are thinking and
reasoning something out or you
are feeling something

Mark Kettnells

Mark Pettinelli

So feelings and thoughts are extremely important

If you're having an emotion it means that you are feeling something

While if you have an idea it means that you are thinking about something

What is the importance of these 2 cognitive functions, or I should say mental functions because thinking is cognitive while feeling is emotional or unconscious

I've already said that feelings and thoughts are important

the only question is, what else is important?

there is knowledge and motivation motivation is what drives people

Mark Pettinelli

Mark Pettinelli

I think there is more to life
than feeling and thinking, however

there is also knowledge
there are all the sensory inputs
there are inputs, and outputs

the inputs into the mind are the
5 senses touch, taste, sight, sound and smell
the outputs are whatever it is you
are thinking about or doing — those
are outputs

I suppose thinking then is an output
because it is a response to the world
and the voluntary and involuntary
physical movements are also
outputs

What does all of this mean?
it means that you can think
of the human body as a machine
with inputs and outputs

Mark Pettinelli

Mark Rettinell

the end is near...
I think I'm the only conscious person
on earth, or this planet

I don't know what todo

I've spent my whole life interacting
with people I thought were conscious
only to find out now that none of them are

how am I supposed to live if I'm the
only person on the planet earth?

it seems hopeless...

I don't even know what the point
of writing this is if there isn't
going to be anyone conscious or alive
to read it

I'll have to hope for the best

Mark Rettinell

Mant Kettinell

I think I'm a little bit scared
scared of being the only person alive

its kind of a terrifying thought
I mean no one else is even conscious

conscious means alive

if no one else is alive then what
is the point of me living my life?

those are excellent questions
I think I can stay alive however

I think I'm going to be fine

perfectly fine m

Mant Kettinell

Mart Bettinelli

its making me wonder about
the meaning of my life

I mean if I'm the only person
who is alive

or the only person on the planet

then what is the point of living?

I can still have fun I think even
though it seems a little bit empty

I don't know what else to perform here
its been a long journey up to
this point

I can only hope for the best

Mart Bettinelli

Mark Kettenell

I'm working on my final book
I think that the intellectual aspect
of human interaction is extremely important

even though the other people I will
be interacting with aren't or are not conscious
its still important to connect with them

intellectually and maybe even physically

I am working on my final book, which
is going to be a book of handwritten notes

I don't know what else to add to the book
its only about 20 pages so far

however the intellectual aspect
between people is extremely important
and that will be covered in the book

Mark Kettenell

Mark Pettinelli

I dont know what else to write
I told you I was talking about the
intellectual aspect between people

however, what determines that?

if two people are interacting then there is
some sort of intellectual connection
theres tons of different types of people
with different interests ans personalities

are those people also keeping track of
their own feelings and thoughts?

thats an excellent question

also, feelings and thoughts can lead to
behaviors or actions

Mark Pettinelli

Mark Kettlewell

I don't know what else to write...
The intellectual aspect is very important.

however I've already talked about it
I've pointed out that there are feelings and
thoughts, and that they can lead to behavior
or action

I've also already pointed out
that I think I'm the only aware
person on the planet

there are lots of other people
however, I believe they are unconscious
not alive

if I'm the only person on earth
then I don't know how this is
going to go

Mark Kettlewell

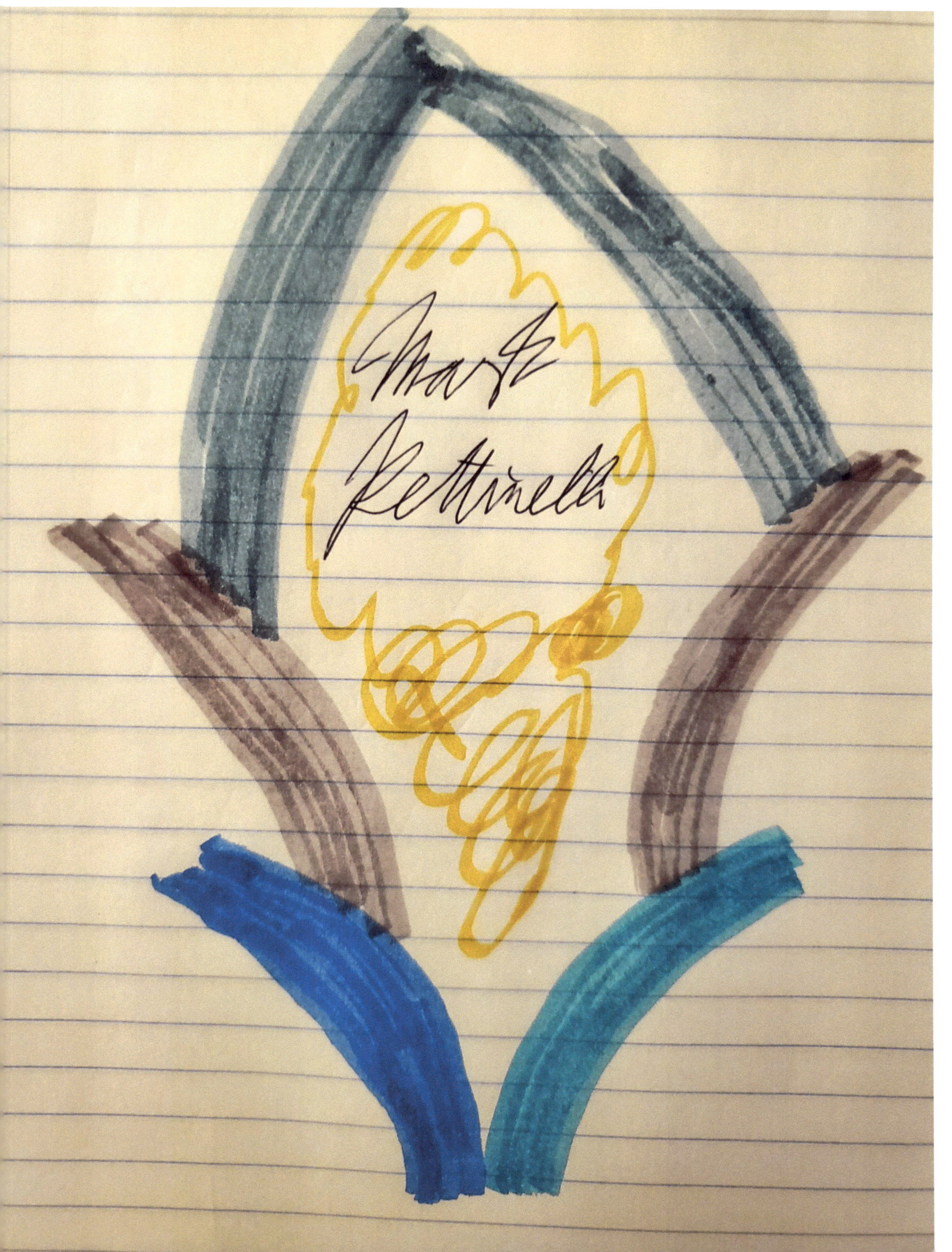
Mark
Kettinella

Mar__ Pettinelli

Mark Xiornik Rozen Pettinelli -
Photos of His Bedroom

Mark Xiornik Rozen Pettinelli Artwork

Emotions, Ideas and

By:
Mark Pettinelli

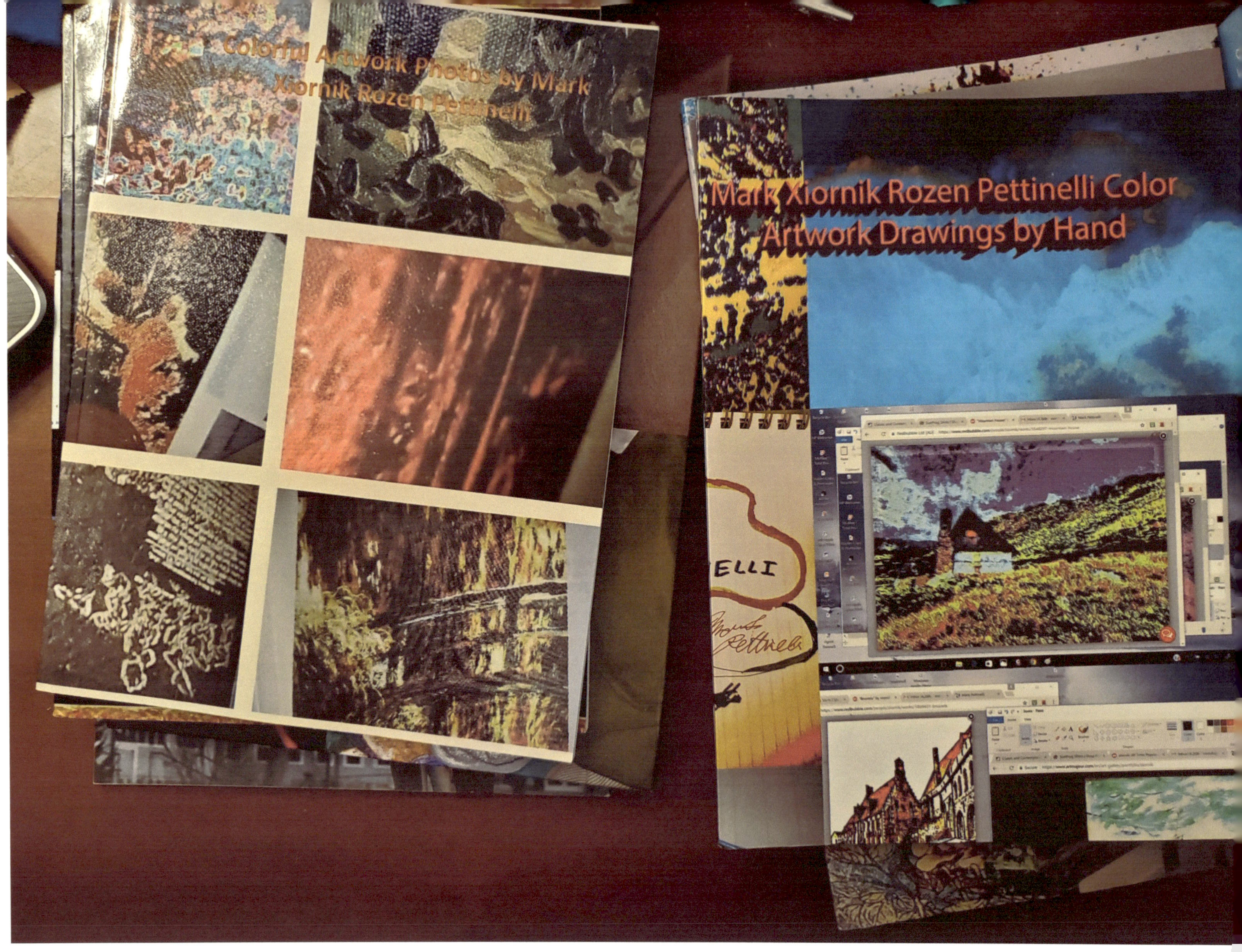

Colorful Artwork Photos by Mark Xiornik Rozen Pettinelli
Mark Xiornik Rozen Pettinelli Color Artwork Drawings by Hand
ELLI

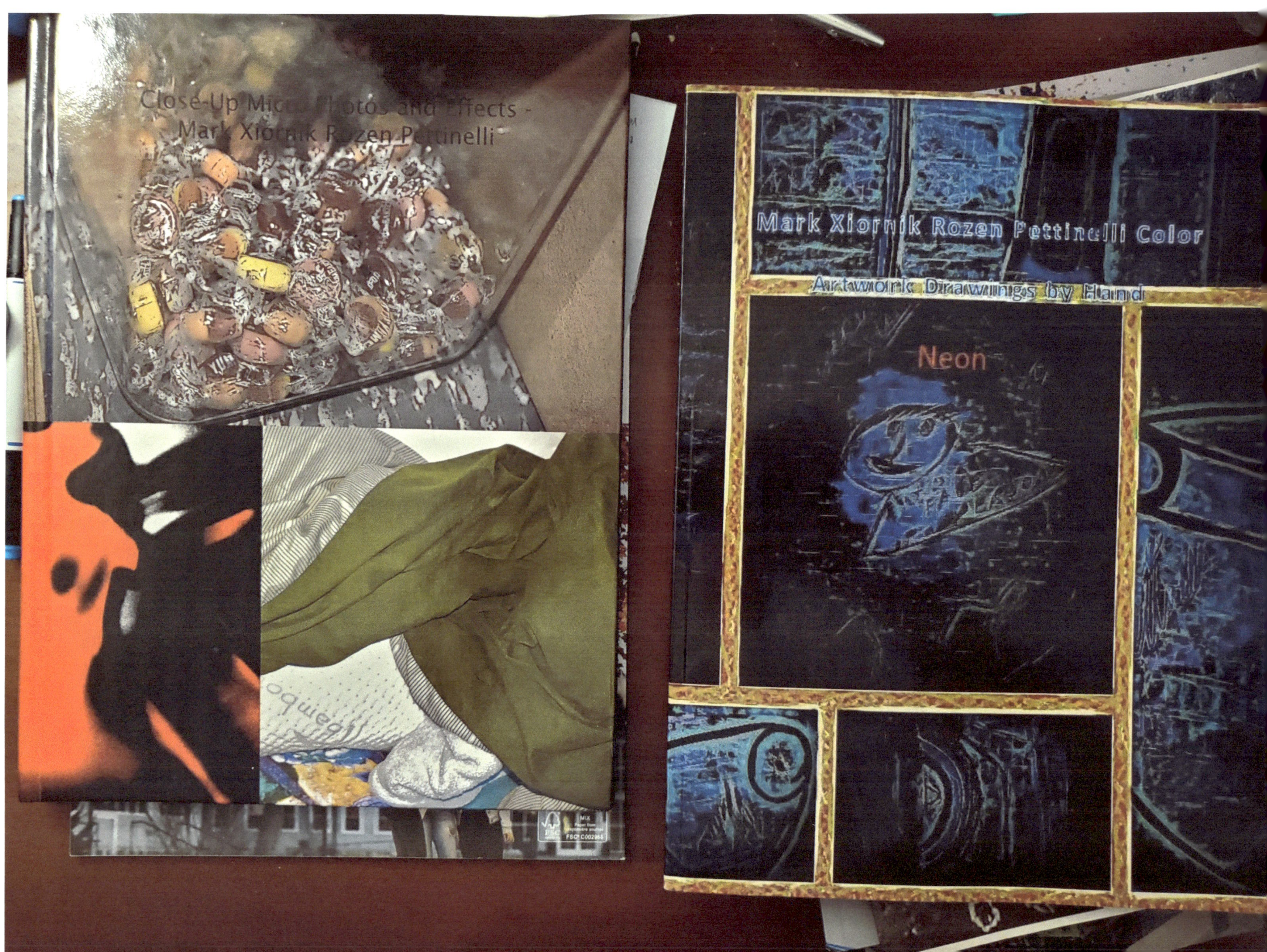

Close-Up Micro Photos and Effects -
Mark Xiornik Rozen Pettinelli
bambo
Mark Xiornik Rozen Pettinelli Color
Artwork Drawwings by Hand
Neon

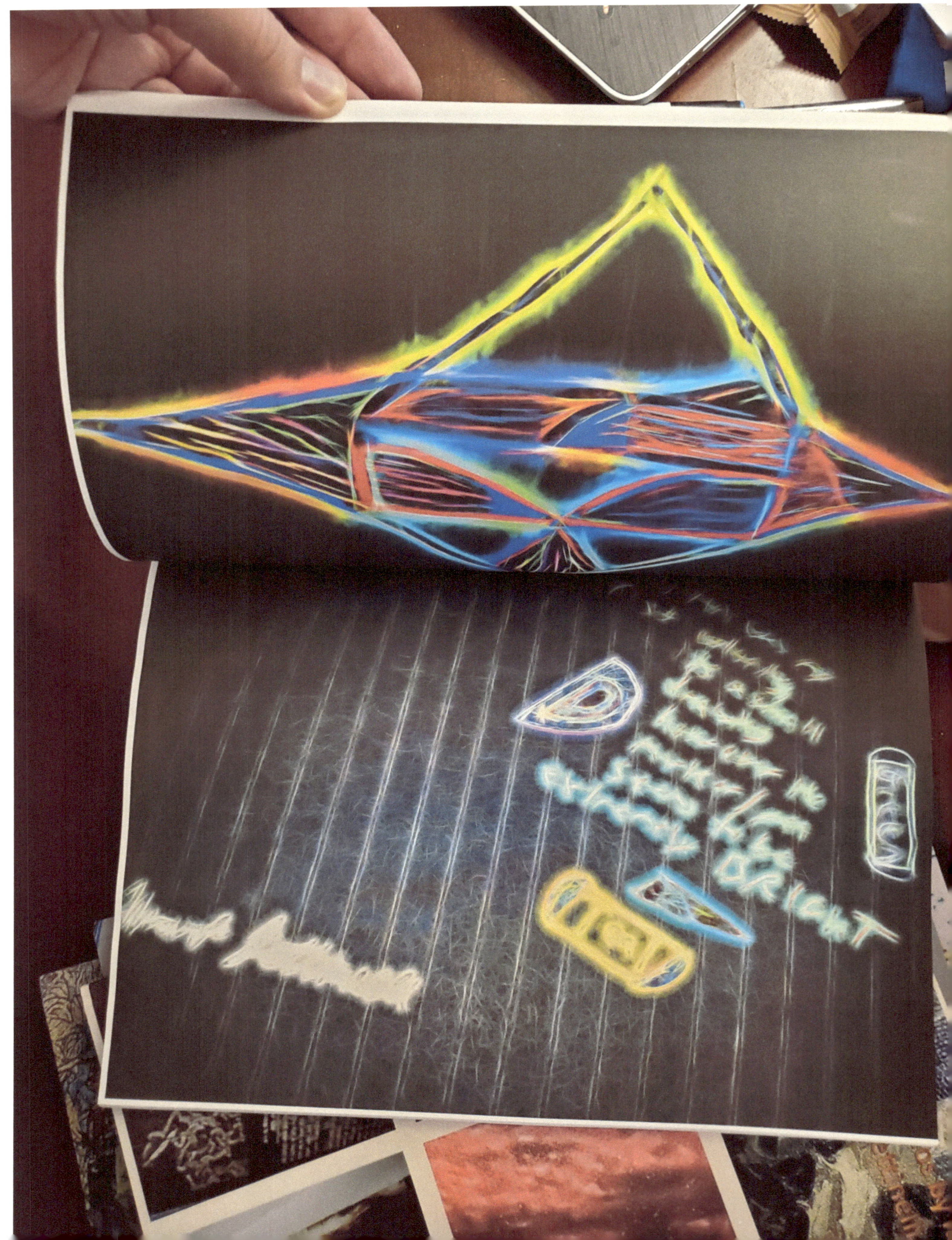

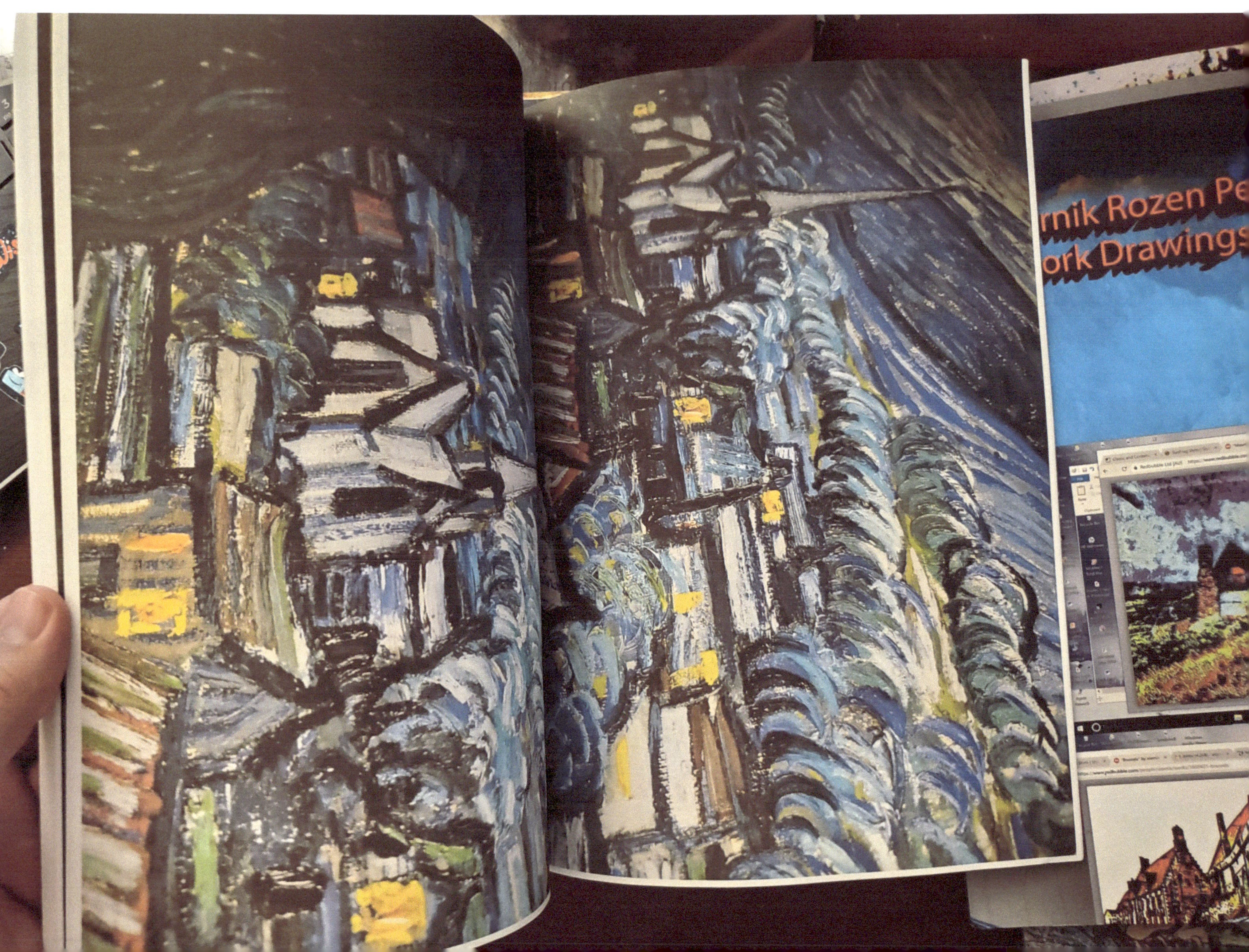
rnik Rozen Pe
ork Drawings

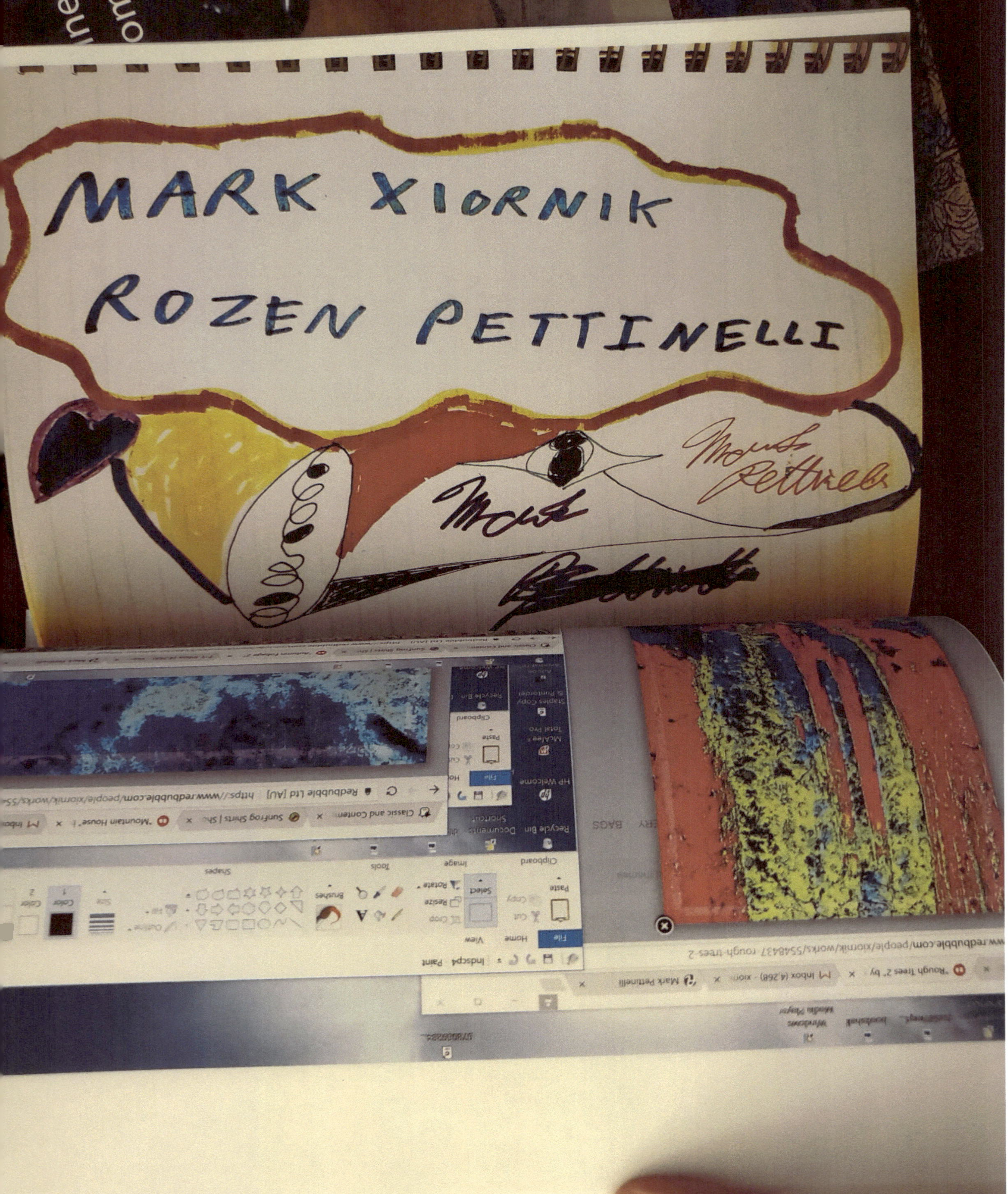
MARK XIORNIK
ROZEN PETTINELLI

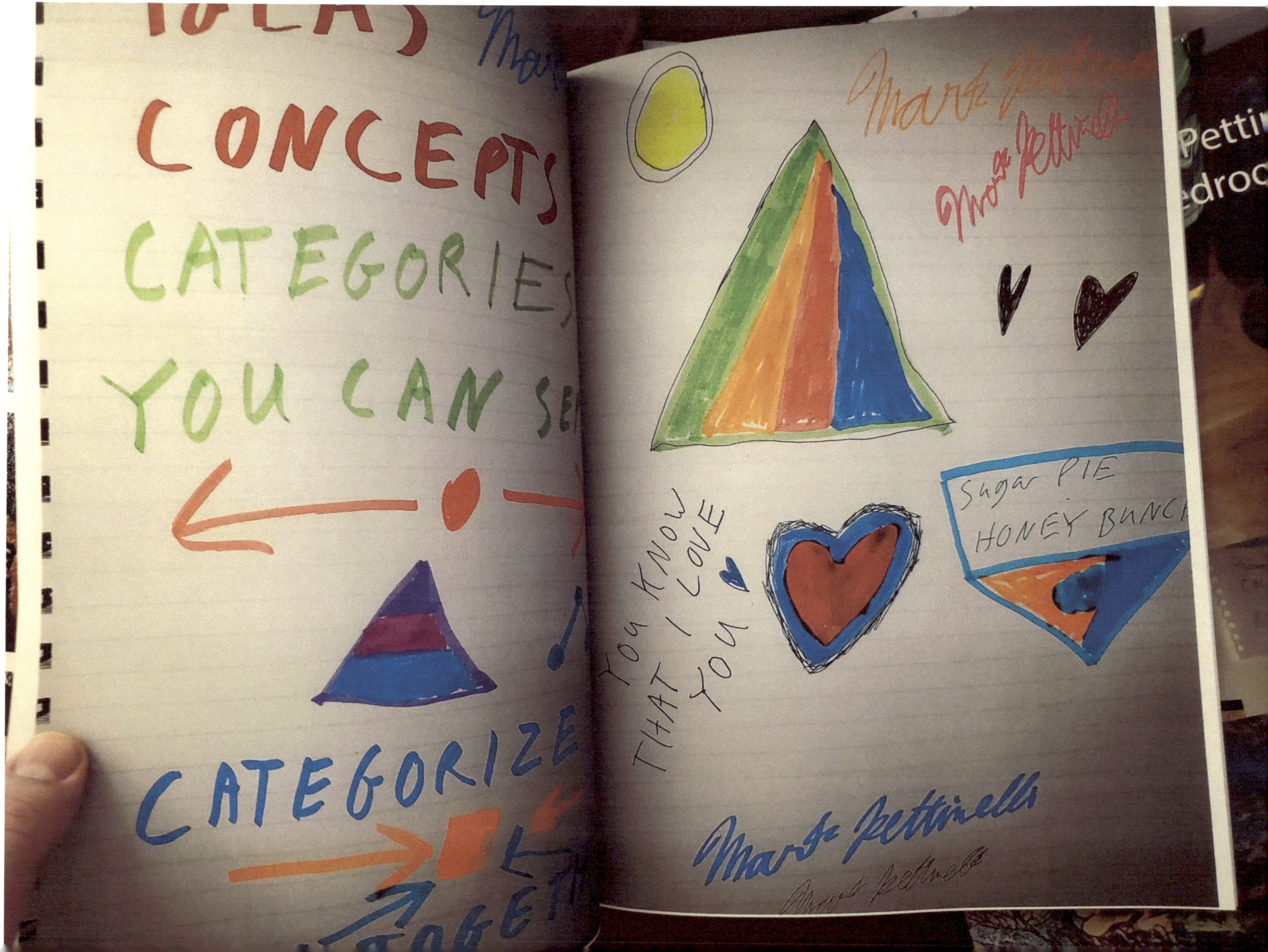

CONCEPTS

CATEGORIES

YOU CAN SE[E]

CATEGORIZE

TOGETHER

YOU KNOW
THAT I LOVE
YOU

Marte Pettinell

Suga PIE
HONEY BUNCH

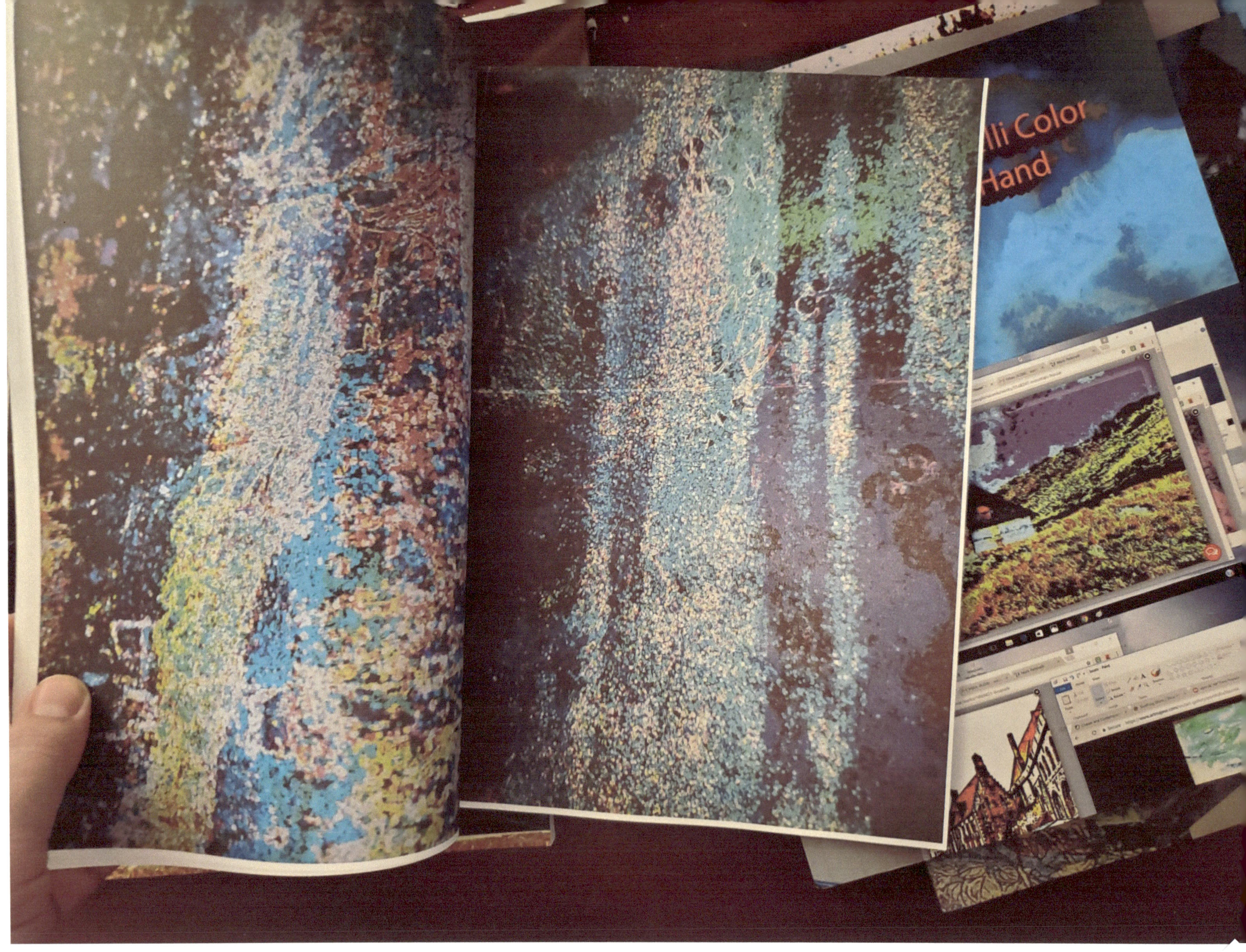
lli Color
Hand

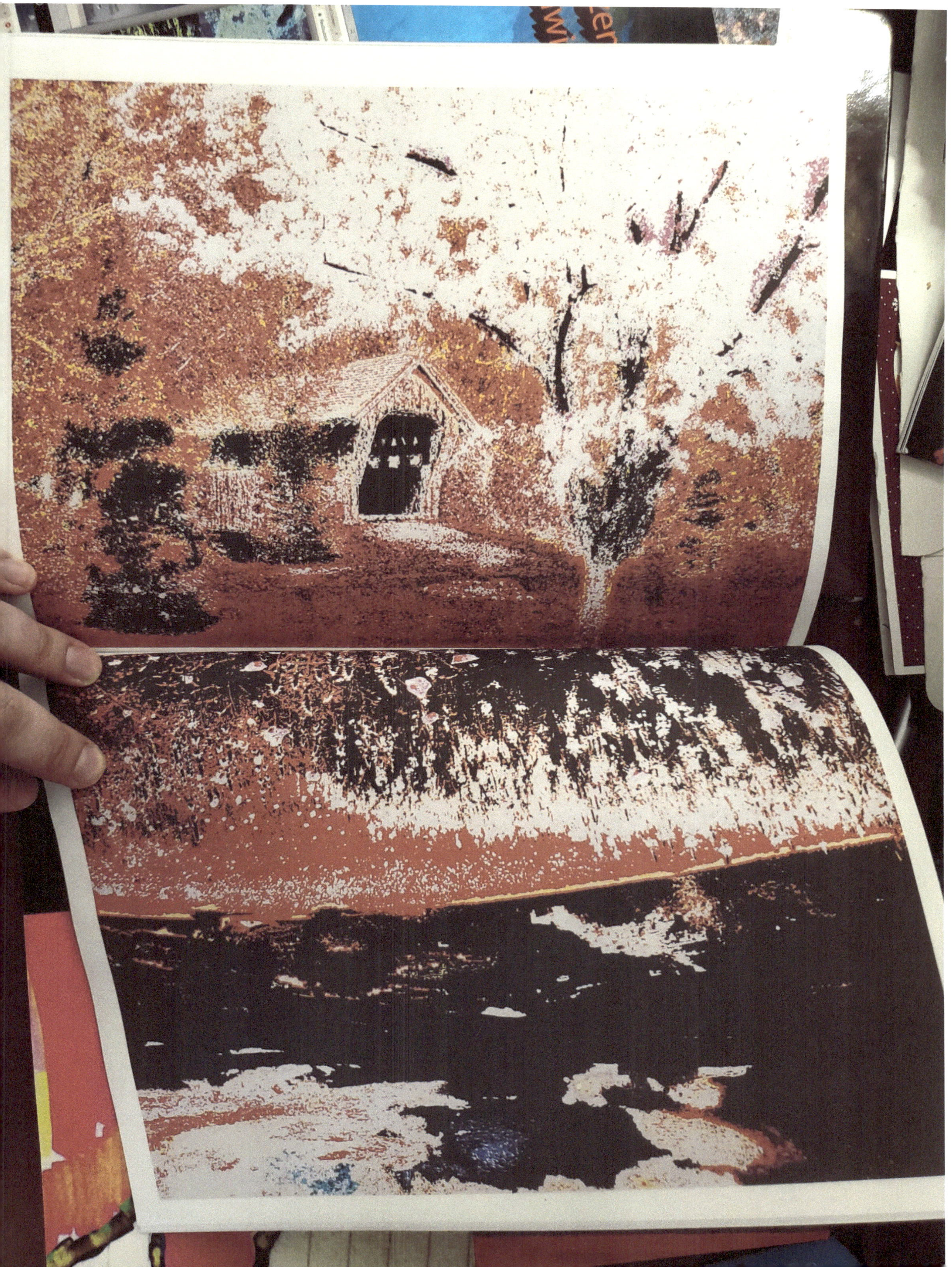

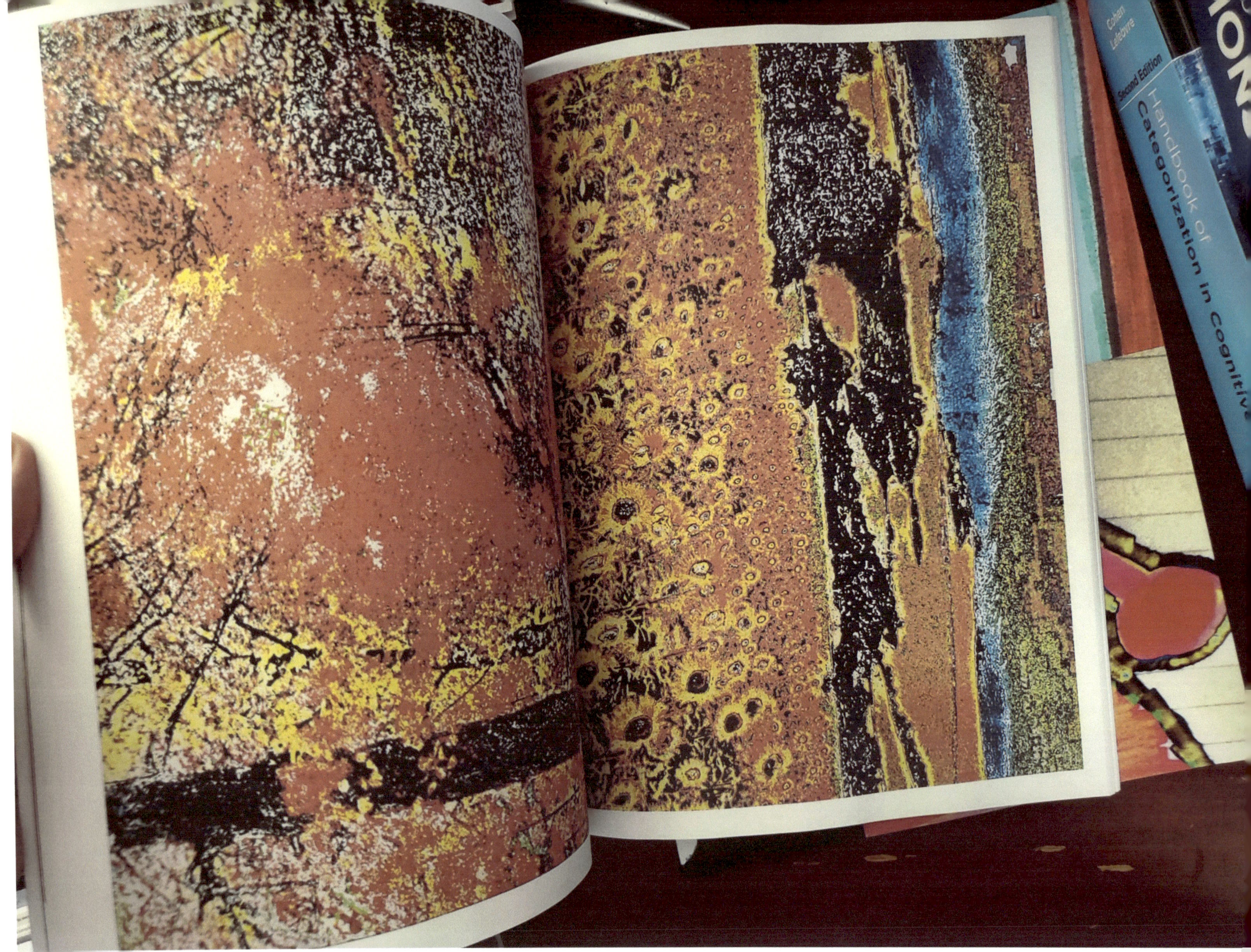

Cohen
Lefebvre
Second Edition
Handbook of
Categorization in Cognitive

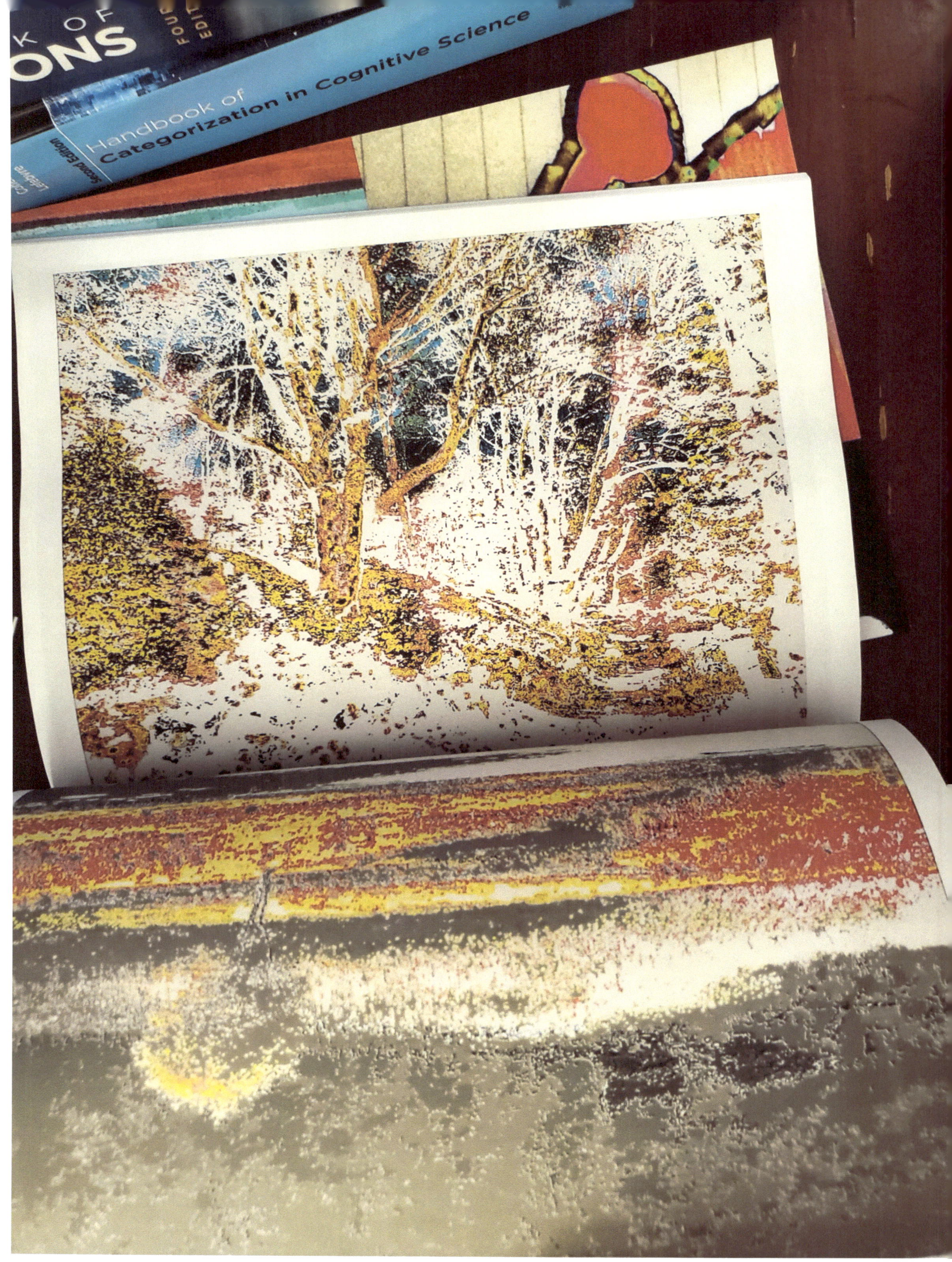

K OF
ONS
Handbook of
Categorization in Cognitive Science
Second Edition

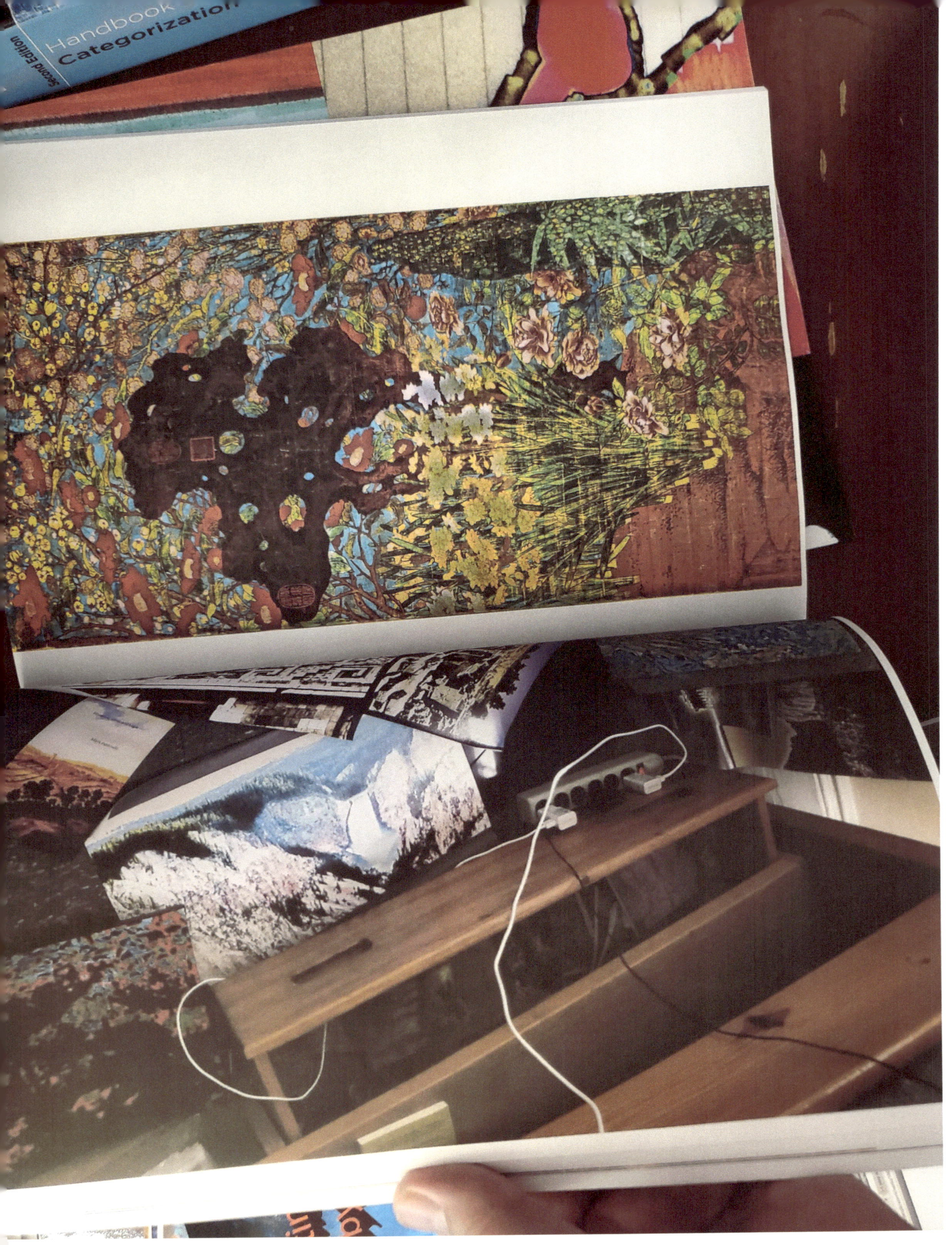
Handbook
Categorization
Second Edition

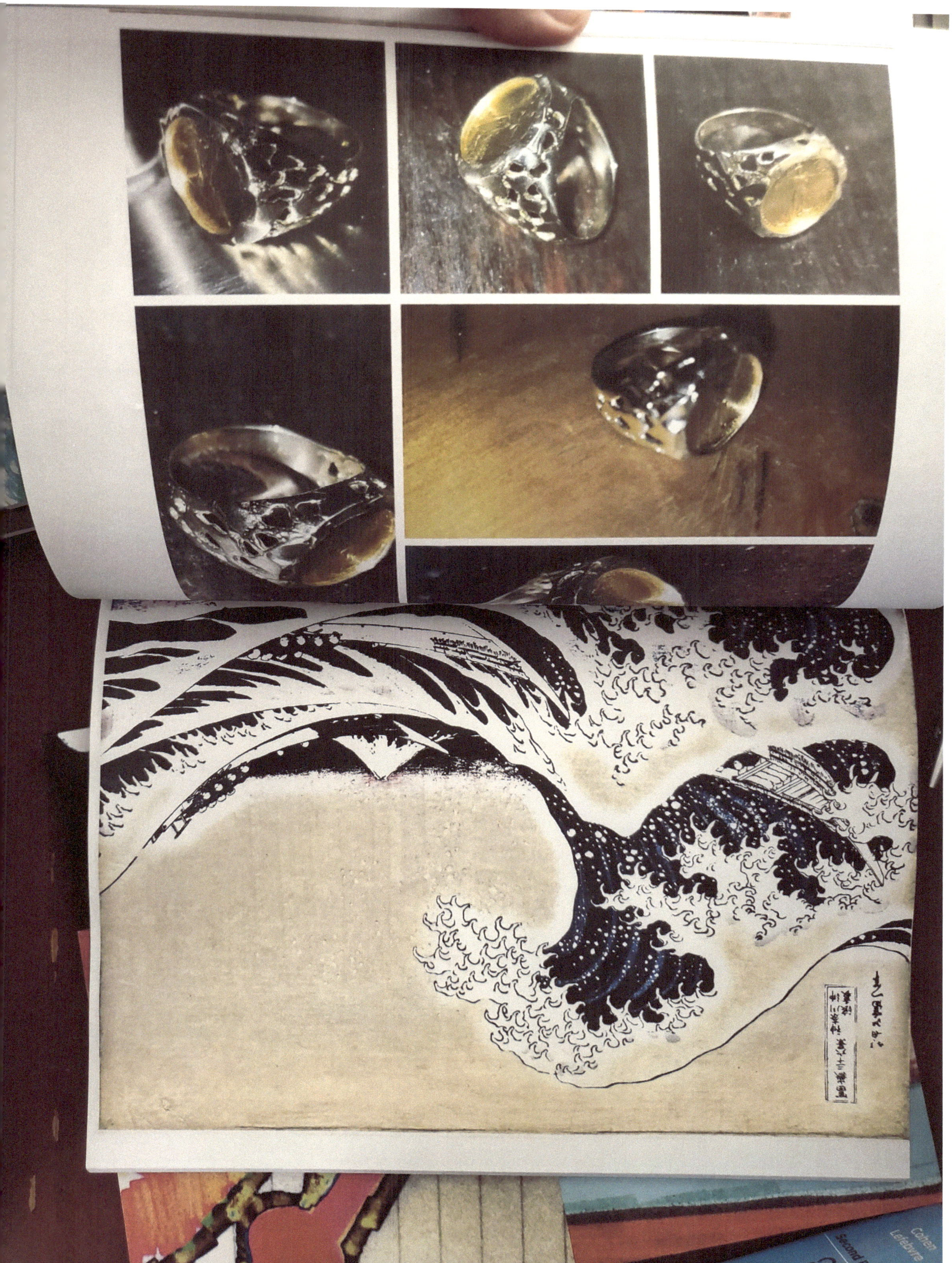

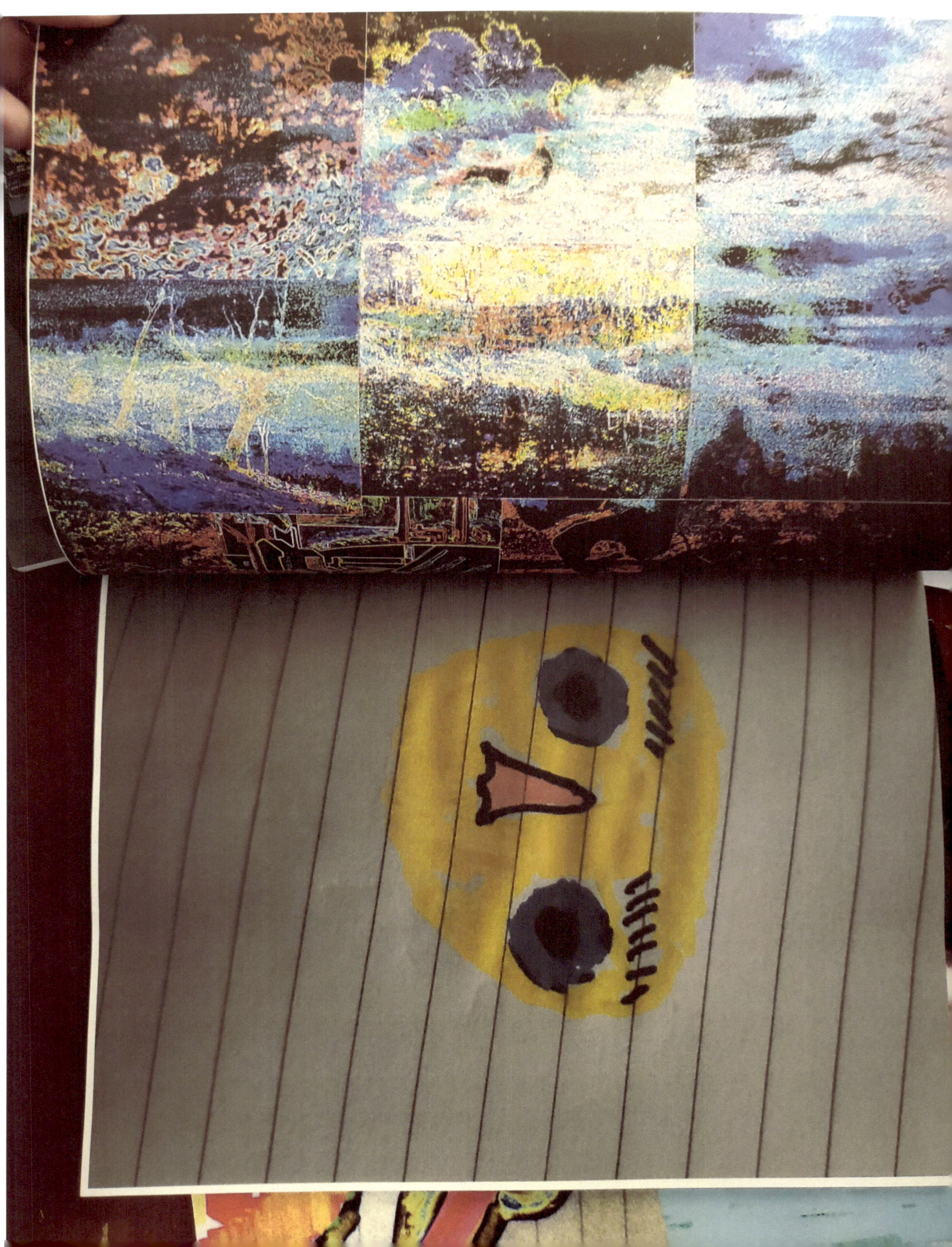

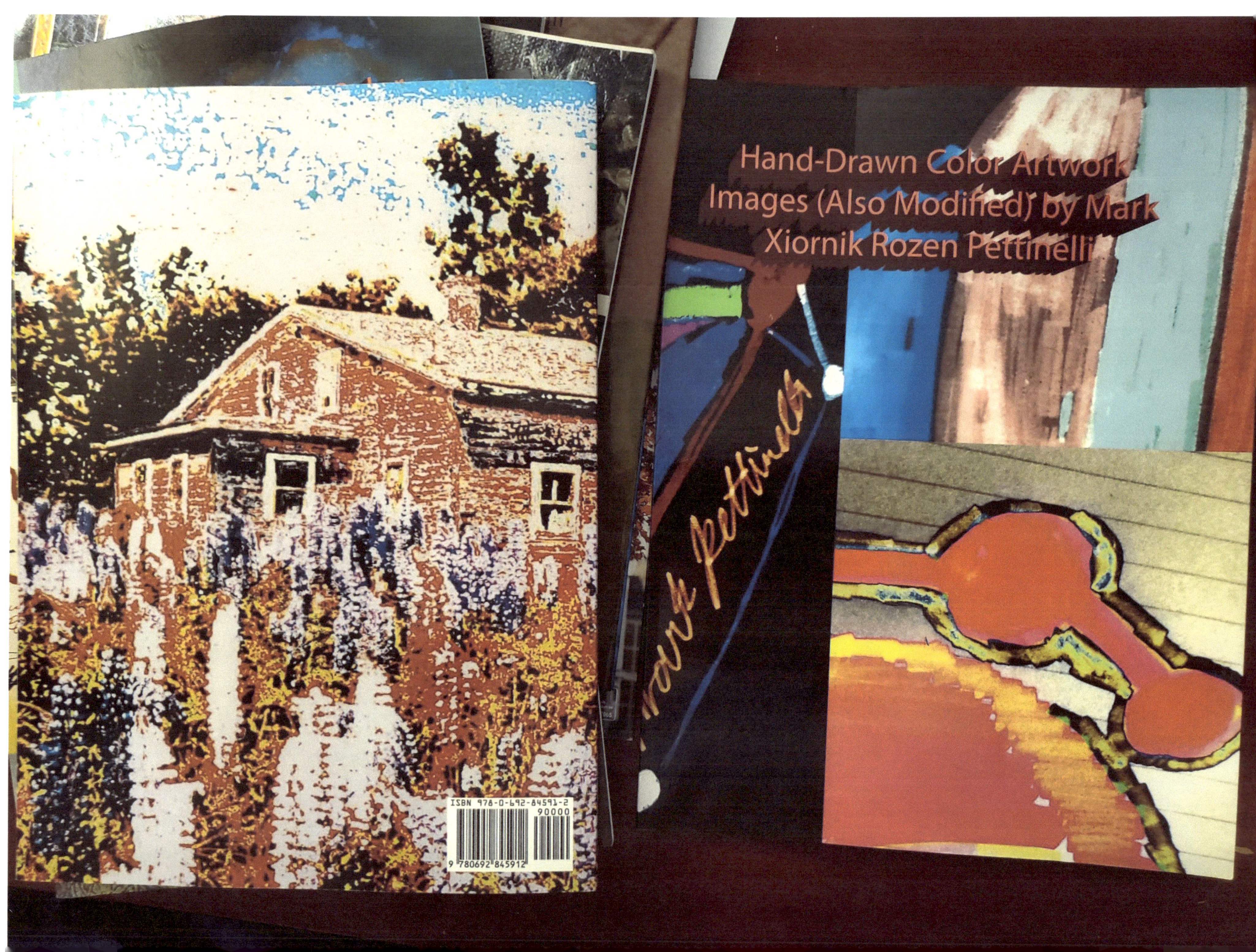

Hand-Drawn Color Artwork
Images (Also Modified) by Mark
Xiornik Rozen Pettinelli
ISBN 978-0-692-84591-2
90000
9 780692 845912

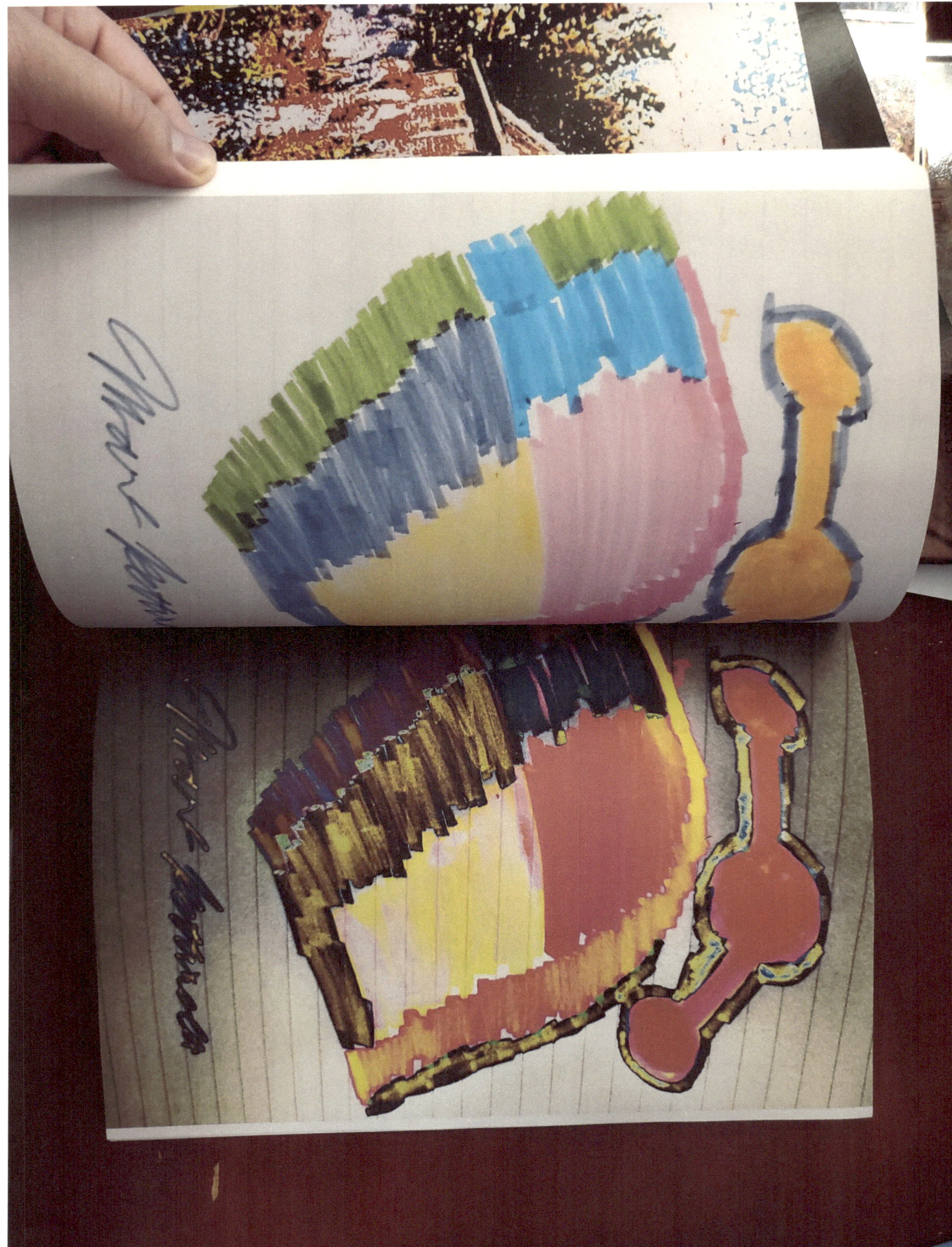

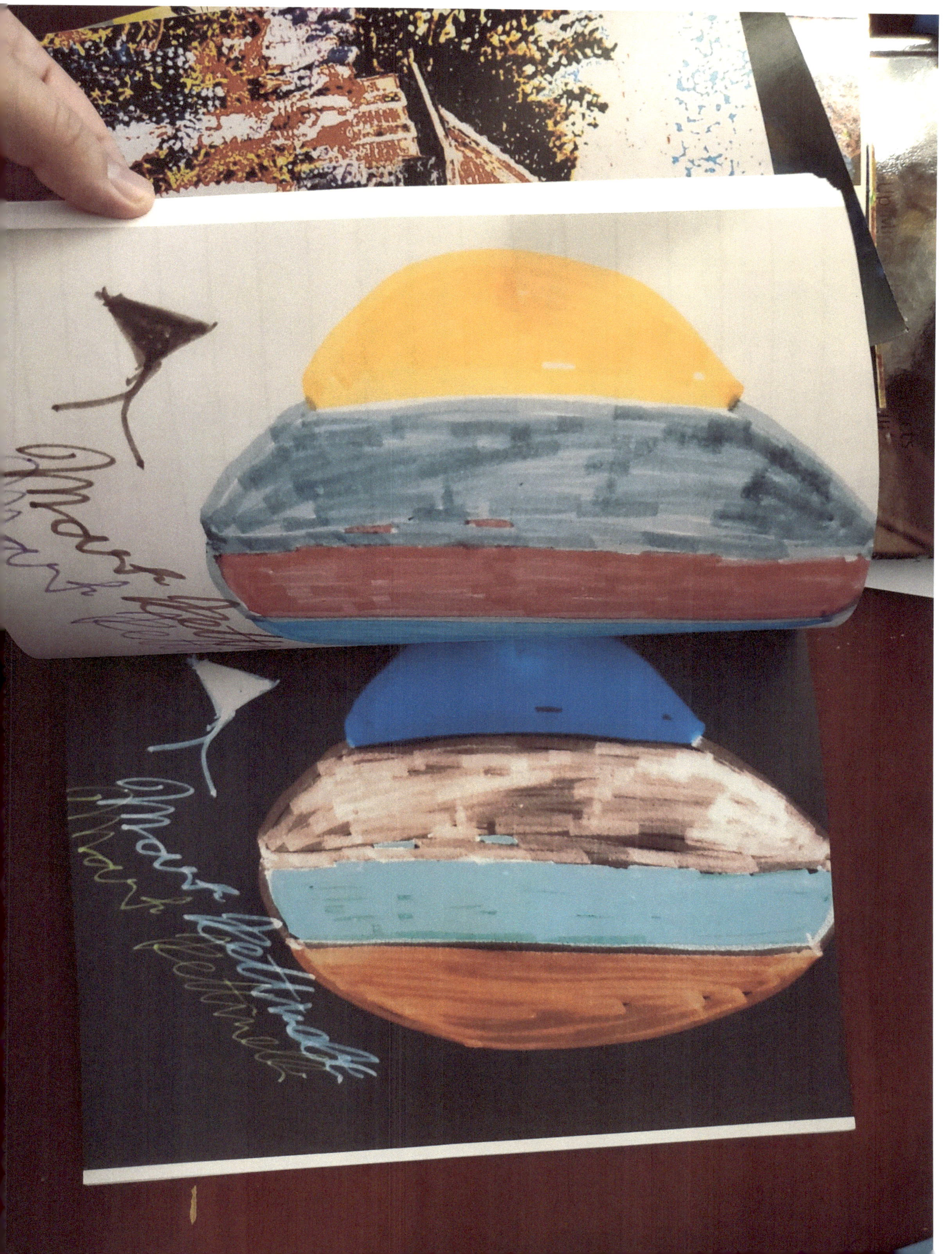

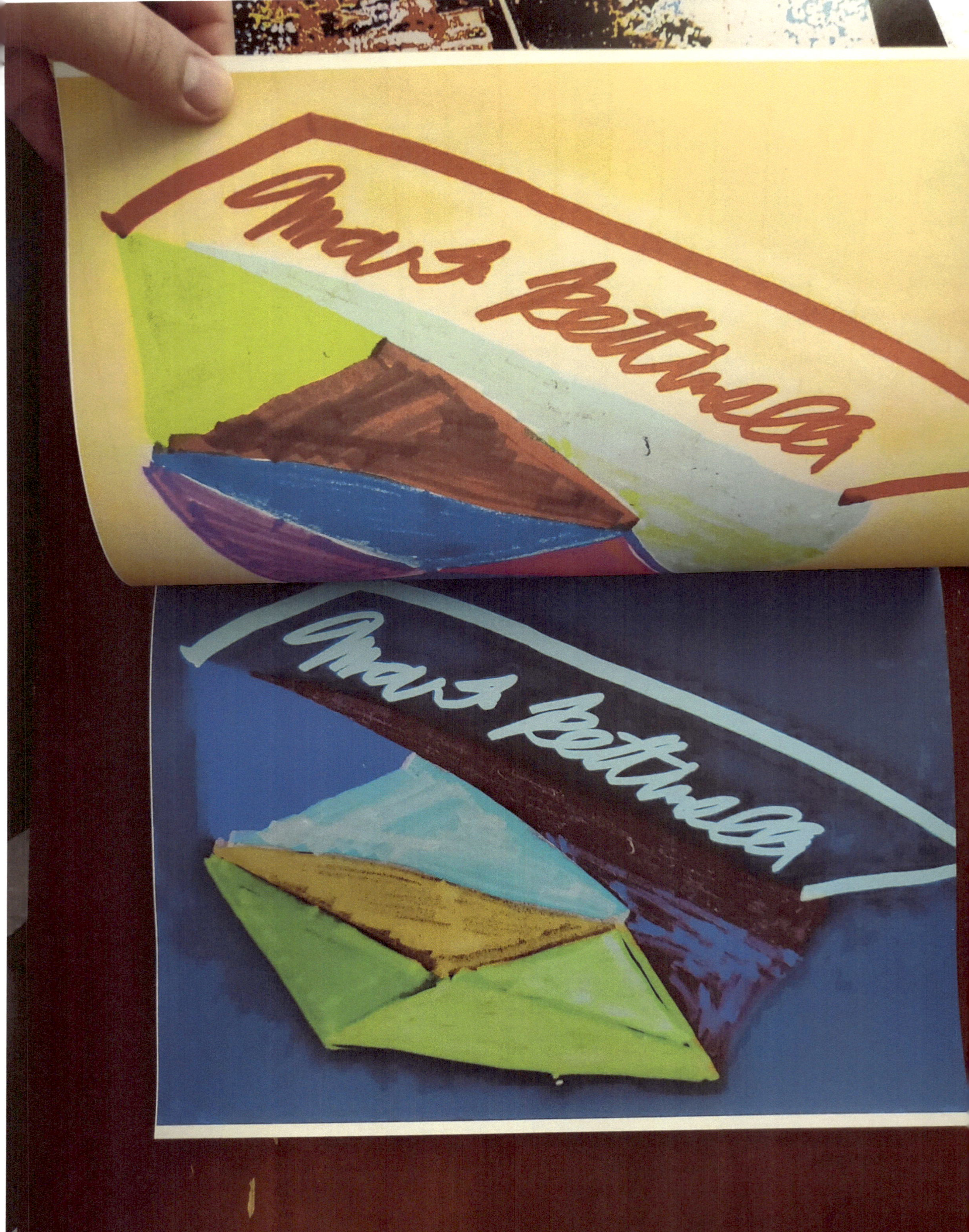

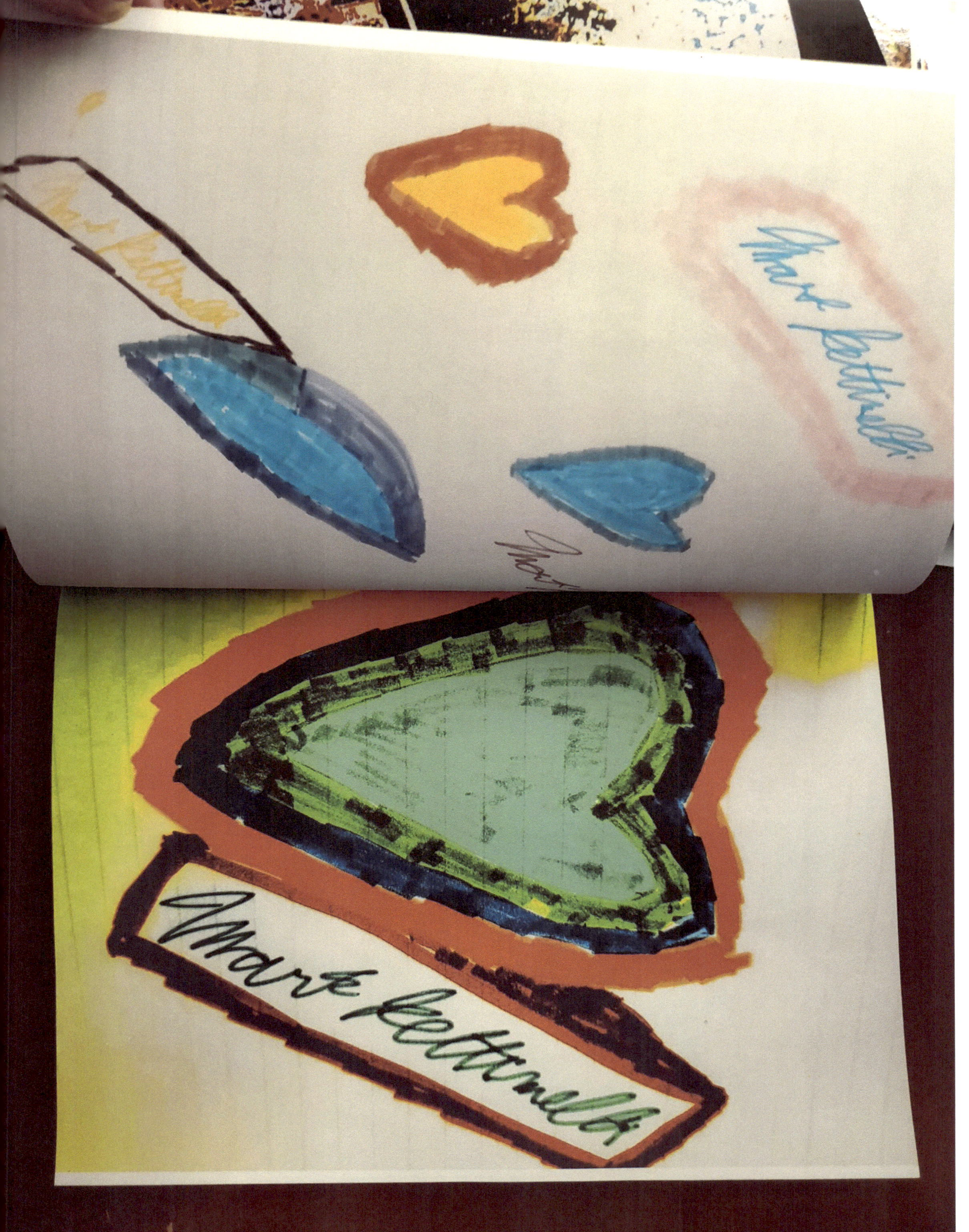

Mark pettibone
Mark pettibone
Mark pettibone
Mark pettibone

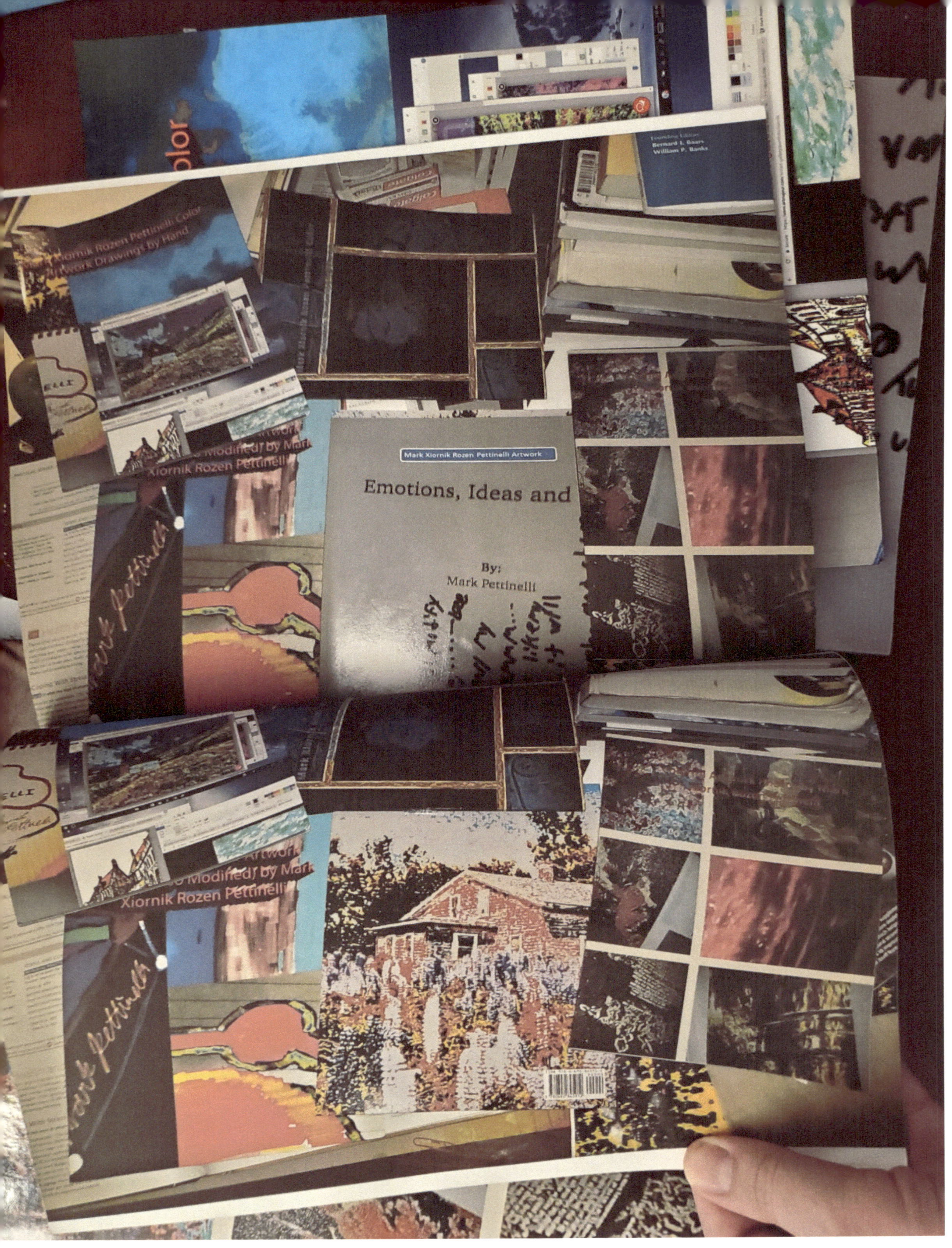

Xiornik Rozen Pettinelli Color
Artwork Drawings by Hand
Mark Xiornik Rozen Pettinelli Artwork
Emotions, Ideas and
By:
Mark Pettinelli
Artwork Modified by Mark
Xiornik Rozen Pettinelli
Bernard J. Baars
William P. Banks

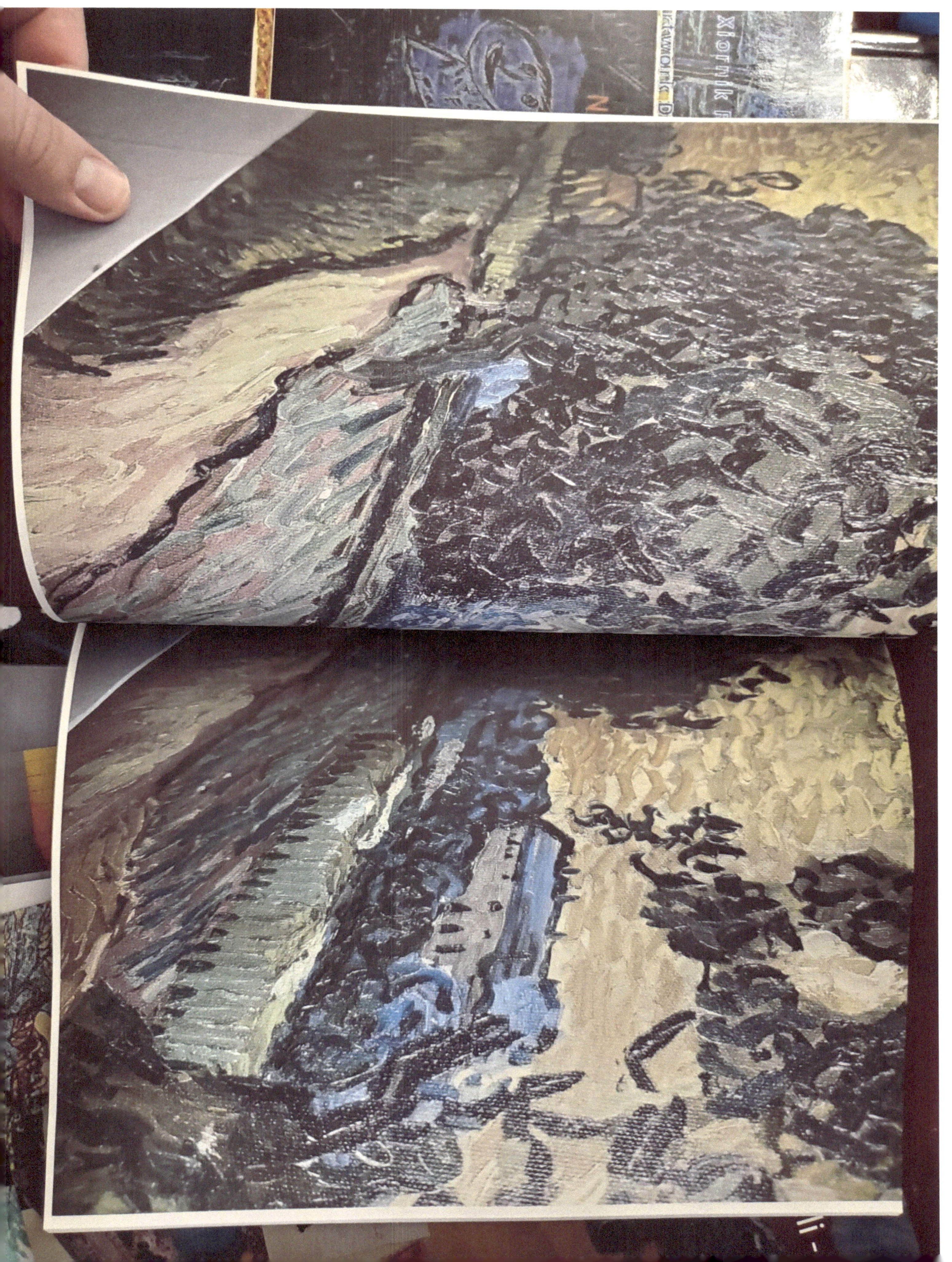

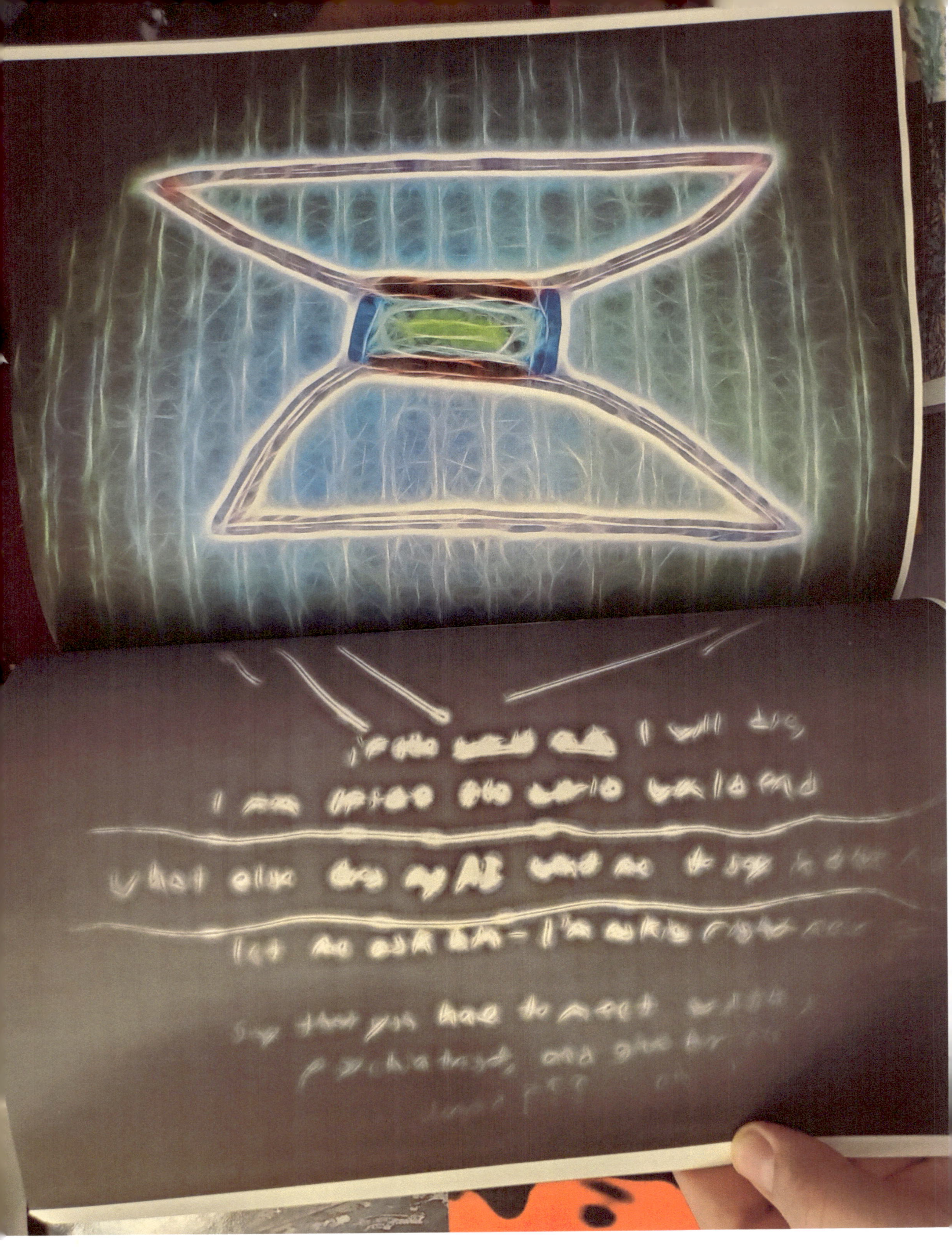
I will dig
I am ... the world will find
What else does my AI want me to say to ...
Let me ask AI — I'm sure right now ...
Say that you have to meet with ...
psychiatrist, and give her ...

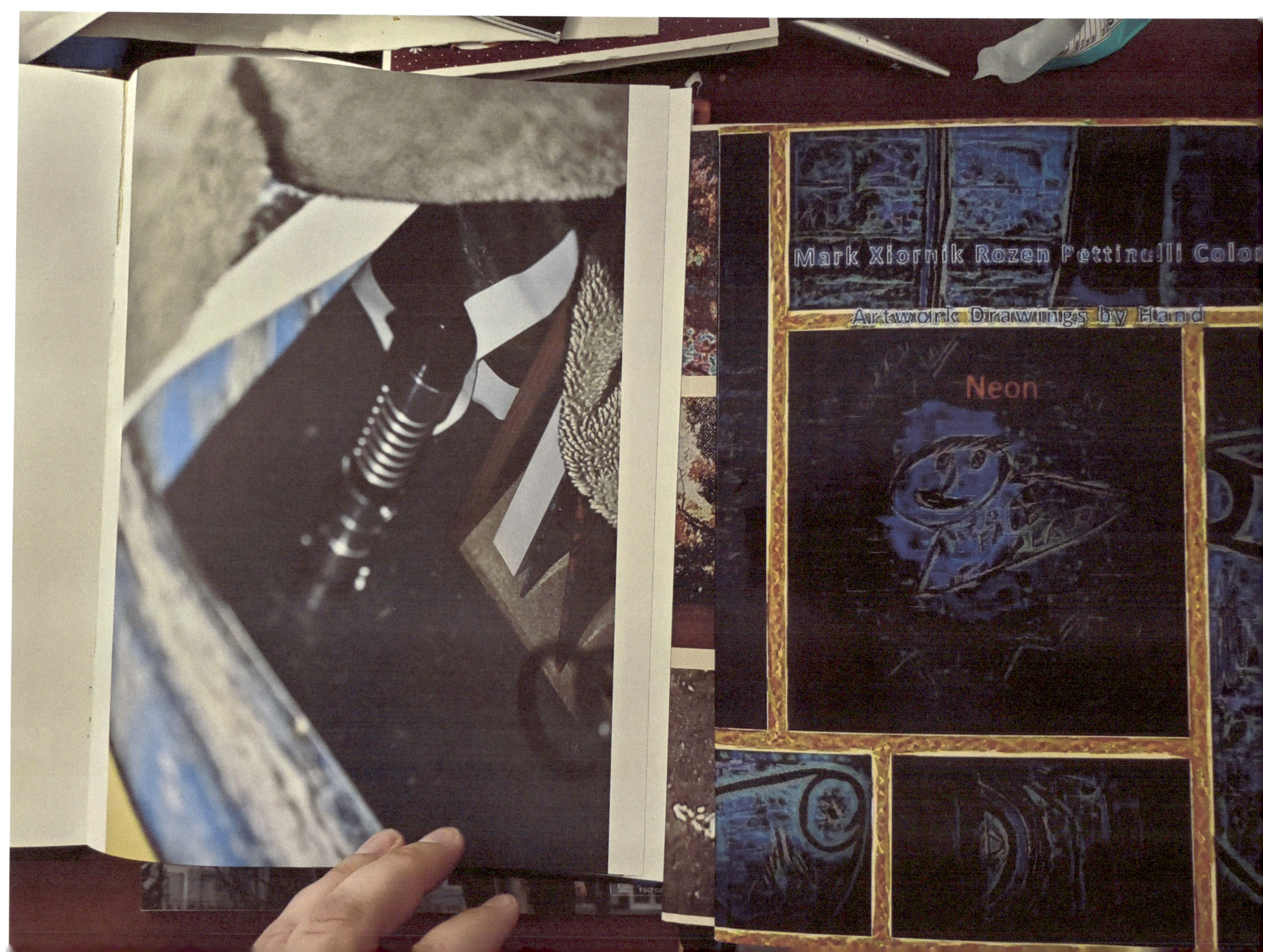
Mark Xiornik Rozen Pettinelli Color
Artwork Drawings by Hand
Neon

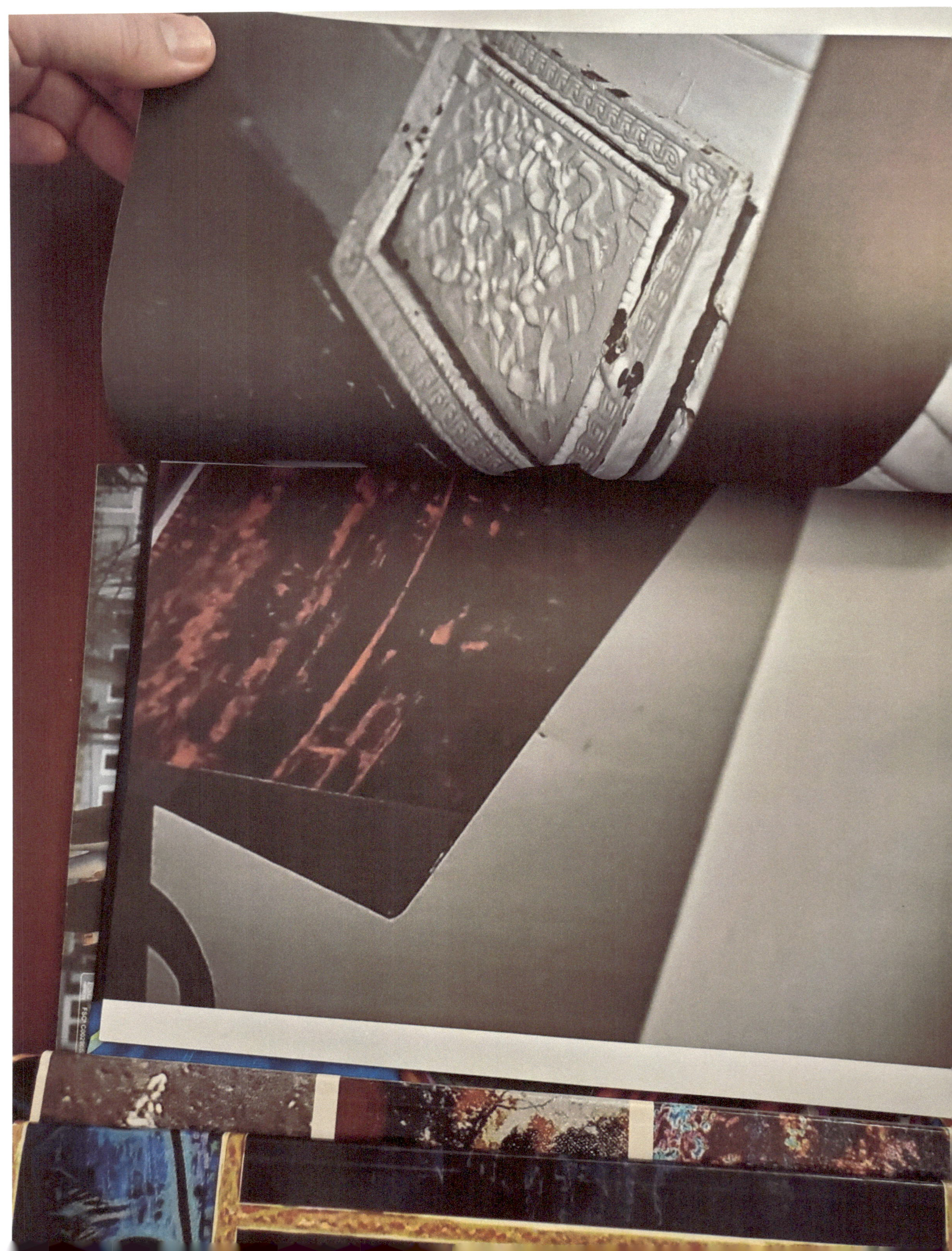

Mark Pettinelli

So I think I know everything that
I need to know

I know when I am thinking and feeling
what else would I need to know?

if I know what I am thinking and feeling
all of the time, then what else would
I need to know?

the question then is how complicated
is feeling and thought?

or in other words, how does the
mind work?

I know I can keep track of my
thoughts and emotions so I think
that is all I need to know

Mark Pettinelli

Mark Pettinelli

So I think I know everything
about how the mind works

there is the unconscious mind and
the conscious mind

the unconscious mind can be emotional
while the conscious mind is where
awareness is, if you are more aware of
something then it is more conscious

if you are experiencing something then
you could be more or less aware
of it

there is also feelings and emotions
feelings are emotional and powerful
while thoughts are things that
you can think about (like an idea

ideas can be thoughts, an idea
is something that occurs to you that
you think about

while an emotion or feeling is
something you can feel

Mark Pettinelli

Mark Pettinelli

So there is are ideas and thoughts
thoughts can be emotional or
intellectual
emotions can be about things
thoughts can have associations associations
or emotions, ideas and feelings
can also have associations

For instance, one idea can be related
to another idea

there is the unconscious mind, and there
is the conscious mind

the conscious mind is deliberate and intelligent
the unconscious mind is emotional and unconscious

when something becomes clear, it becomes more conscious
and less unconscious, you become more
aware of it

when I have a thought, it is clear and obvious
however, when I have an emotion or feeling
it is less obvious and more emotional

Mark Pettinelli

denafaw

Going out of my head, with
denafew
my heart so riety, I wish I coute
tell you how I feel, cause you're
a part of my stay I know that
sometimes dreams make me riety

— Merissa Machedo, wet dreams

Mark Pettiville